Of Meadows and Flowers -

and Crying  and Hope

ISBN: 1463770030
ISBN-13: 978-1463770037

Table of Contents

Preface

"Being a kid is tough," were the words my father said to me as he handed me what would turn out to be one of my most favorite books. I read it so many times that the cover fell off and I had to tape it back on. It was getting near the end of middle school, so I had already figured out on my own that being a kid really can be tough. Some of these poems come from that time. Others I wrote while in high school and into college. They were all written during times when I struggled to hold onto my sanity—or as I tried to cope when I couldn't.

There are lots of important books out there. I hope this will become one of them. Perhaps a teen will stumble on it when they are having a difficult time. Or maybe a parent or friend will hand it to someone they love and say, "Being a kid is tough." My dream is that you will read this book so many times that the cover falls off.

This is a book about crying. About hearing voices. About being lonely. But, most of all, it's about hope. Hope is something I have, and I hope that after reading this book, you will know that even if you want to scream or cry or cut or die, that life is always something worth looking forward to. 🦋

Of Meadows and Flowers - and Crying and Hope

PATRICIA LARSTED

Is It Normal?

Is it normal?
To not want to bring
A child
Into this world
Because I don't want
My offspring
To have to go through
What I've been through?
Is it normal?
To write a sad poem
So I can cry through my words
Because I can't
Cry through my eyes?
Is it normal?
To count down from ten
Hoping that somehow
It will comfort me?
Is it normal?
To draw a butterfly on my wrist
As a device
To keep from slitting it?
Is it normal?
To have to fight
To pay attention
Against the voices
Who are screaming in my head?
Is it normal?
To wonder
If it's normal
To
Be
Like
Me?

I've always wondered about normalcy. Is it really worth trying to fit in, when I know I never will?

I Left Everything in My Room

I left everything in my room
Perfect
So someone could find anything I asked for
With as few directions as possible.
I left everything in my mind
Perfect
Everything all set
Strong opinions with strong foundations
Tripods, not stakes.
I knew what I knew
Very little, at that
I knew what I wanted to know
And how to ask for it.
I knew nothing about my situation
So I tried to sort through the facts
For what was necessary to know
To know just what was going on.
How much help do I need?
Will they tell me to handle it on my own?
Will I have to be the one to break the news to my friends
That I was ripping apart our plans?
Ripping the sturdy foundation down
That we had spent so much time building up.
My classes?
What would become of them
In the lost time?
My life?
My plans?
My friends?
I knew what I knew:
Nothing.
And in the nothingness
Comes uncertainty.
Unstable footing.
My strong base demolished.
And maybe,
Though my current state was fine,
My life and my past would lead people to think
That I wasn't okay on my own. ⟶

Am I okay?
Will I be okay?
Time will tell
But I hope the answer is yes.

I wrote this in the hospital. I wasn't sure enough that I was going to end up there to pack a bag, but I left my room in a state that someone else could pack one for me.

Bandaged Brain

Ignoring the pain
Going insane
Thoughts down the drain
My bandaged brain.

Thinking too fast
Healing too slow
Feeling the pain
My bandaged brain.

Forcing a smile
Over a frown
Healing the lame
My bandaged brain.

Trying to be strong
Sick of the weak
Going insane
My bandaged brain.

Trying too hard
To harbor a smile
A crutch or a cane
My bandaged brain.

Ignoring the pain
Going insane
Thoughts down the drain
My bandaged brain.

I wrote this when I was thinking lots of random thoughts and wanted to bandage my brain to stop the unnecessary thoughts from rushing in. My metaphorical bandage was medication, which I try not to rely on, but it does work.

Please Dad

Please, Dad. Help me.
Dry my tears.
Please, Dad. Help me.
Sedate my fears.

Please, Dad. Help me.
I can't stop crying.
Please, Dad. Help me.
I'm afraid of dying.

Dad, dear. Save me.
I feel so lost.
Dad, please. Save me.
Whatever the cost.

I'm sad and crying.
I just can't stop.
I'm really not lying.
This poem's a flop.

My father is my hero. He's always there for me. He is my savior. He calms me. He dries my tears. He's the greatest. When I'm crying or upset he will embrace me until I feel happy and safe.

Free Verse

If you go to the library
And look for just a minute,
You'll find that there are
Far too many books
About writing assignments
At school.
Being a student myself
I agree,
And I wonder
Why teachers give
Writing assignments
In the first place.
But when I complain,
Like in the books,
They say they're preparing me
For
My
Future.
Some future that requires me
To write a diamante poem
Or a personal narrative.
Come to think of it...
What kind of future will require me
To calculate
How many white shoes
And black shoes
Are made
Just by knowing
– How much one of each color costs
– How many shoes there were total
– And the total profit
That's what bookkeeping is for.

So anyway, I was happy today.
Not usually,
Just today.
Because my English teacher told me
That I had to write
A free-verse poem.
How wonderful.
The sun felt a little warmer.
The bells rung a little sooner.

And I'm wearing a smile
Because I'm free.

Oh dear,
I don't like this at all.
What kind of free-verse poem is it
If you *have* to include a simile:
This school is like hell,
Or a metaphor:
The devil constricts my poetry,
Or maybe an alliteration:
Swords slice the silence.
How is that free verse?
When I'm not free to write what I want?
And just what *I* want?
Not all of these strange, slithering, stupid
Constrictions on what I write?
Because it's what I write.

What
I
Write.

Not my teacher.
Not my mother.
Just me, and I'm the only one who should care.
Not my teacher.
Not my mother.

But unfortunately, this isn't a perfect world.
My teacher has a say.
My mother, well, she can say what she wants.

But isn't it ironic
That a free-verse poem
Would shackle me down?

Every time a teacher tells me we're going to do a unit on poetry I get excited, until I figure out that I won't be writing about anything I want, but will be shackled down by what the teacher wants.

Patricia

Pretending to be
Alright is not really worth the
Time because I know people can see I'm
Really sad
Inside
'Cause even when
I say I
Am okay, I, at least, know I am not.

I write acrostic poems for people on holidays, like Mother's Day and birthdays, and I usually use the recipient's name. Mine is the only one I decided to include.

Petals

I love him
Don't I?
I need him
Don't I?
He loves me...
He loves me not...
I shouldn't have to decide my fate with a simple flower
Ripping its beauty apart
Petal by petal
Is all this just ripping me up?
Is it worth it?
Am I sure I'm on solid ground?
And if I'm swept off my feet
I hope it's by him loving me
Not the rapids of life knocking me down
Will it be by him?
I don't know

She cares
Doesn't she?
Say prayers
That she does
The way she looks at me
The way she looks at me
I can't ignore it
I must ignore it
How can I go on with this uncertainty?
I know she feels for me as I feel for her
Why doesn't she come tell me?
Why?
Why don't I tell her how I feel?
Because I do feel
And my feet, they're cold
My hands, they sweat
My eyes, they soak up her beauty
Like lips drawing liquid from a glass
The way she looks at me
Through the side of her eye
A backwards glance ⟶

Is that good?
Is that bad?
It is good…
Maybe

But I hope the answer is yes

But I hope the answer is yes

Unrequited love is a common theme in my poetry. I have never been completely head over heels in love, but I'm far too used to having crushes not care back. I hope I never have things go as badly as they do in some of my poems.

The Walls Are Blue

The walls are blue
A strange shade at that
Kind of like a robin's egg
With just a touch of sky
On a perfect summer day
Is it a perfect color, then?
I think not
Just because perfection is mixed into something
Doesn't mean it has to be anywhere near perfect
The color is awful
I'm glad it's not on my walls

The ceiling's weird
Those tiles?
They're not all the same color
Maybe it's supposed to be a pattern
If it is, it's a lame one
Four sprinklers to save us all
Lucky us
There are funny lights hanging from the ceiling
I like the florescent lights better
There are weird things on the walls
Weird things on weird walls
The color brown could be a bird's nest
Robin's eggs on a robin's nest
What a concept

Although this room is strange
Is there a possibility that someone finds joy
In calling this room their own?
Maybe, maybe not
But I hope the answer is yes

Class can get very boring. When it does, I tend to notice small details, like the colors of the walls and the patterns on the ceiling. I wonder about perfection a lot. Is it worth the effort? I think not.

My Stone Grey Eyes

They tell me they're beautiful
My sky blue eyes
They say eyes like mine
Draw people's attention
From the freckles that dot my face
More freckles than grains of sand
On the beach
In summer
Where the sky is blue
Beautiful blue
Like my eyes
They say my eyes
Have a deep and rich color blue
More than the sky
They say the sky doesn't compare
To my beautiful eyes
They say that looking inside my eyes
All you can see is hope
And a twinkle like a star
My sky blue eyes
But they don't see
Those times
When I lock myself
In my room
And cry
And my eyes
My sky blue eyes
With hope inside
Are gone
And I'm left with
My stone grey eyes
And the freckles on my face
More freckles than stars in the sky
On a pitch black night
In summer
And through my stone grey eyes
I look out
At your olive eyes
Staring back at my clouded stone eyes
And I don't care how many people tell me
My eyes are beautiful ⟶

And I don't care how many people don't tell you
Your eyes are beautiful
Because your eyes are beautiful
Reflected
In my
Stone
Gray
Eyes 🦋

I wrote this during my first hospitalization when I made a friend who helped me through a difficult time. Unfortunately we haven't kept in touch, but I imagine him and his beautiful eyes when I need a friend and can't find one.

A Funeral for My Sanity

A funeral for my sanity
Will you please comfort me?

Painful tears stream down my face
Will you help me leave this place?

Why do I feel so alone,
Like a dog without her bone?

While I feel the days go by
Why do I so want to die?

Dripping blood is in my mind
Help me to make my stress unwind.

Why can I not find a friend?
When will I finally meet my end?

I really don't want to die
As I watch these days go by.

A song repeats inside my head
I so want to go to bed.

I hear voices others can't
My roots are weak, unlike a plant.

A funeral for my sanity
Please, oh please, comfort me.

Med changes are a common occurrence for me. When I wrote this, I was slowly weaning myself off a particularly nasty medication. This med change sparked many poems. I wonder why when I feel awful, one of the first thoughts to go through my head is "I want to die." I really don't want to die. Life is a gift, and I shouldn't treat it fickly.

Crying Through My Words

Crying through my words is something I
Really try not to do, but as the
Years go by
I find myself crying more and more, but to
No avail, I still feel awful.
Gee, I guess

There is some way I could stop
Hoarding these words in my
Roundabout way,
Over here! Me! Please stop to notice me, ignore my
Uglier features. Perhaps some
Good will come out of this self-inflicted
Hell that

My mind is stuck in. As the
Years go by I cry through my

Words. Over and
Over again, I'm hoarding these words in my
Roundabout way. Oh,
Dear. I'm repeating myself. And all that I'm creating is
Sadness.

I often find that I really want to cry. I know it would make me feel better, but tears won't come. When this happens I cry through my words. This is an example of one of my acrostic poems, where the first letter of every line spells out a word or phrase.

Ashamed

Somehow my dog knows.
When I call for her,
Leash in hand.
She knows that instead of yelling at her,
Telling her to get out of the poison ivy
That I will be talking
To the people
No one else can hear.
No one else can feel.
The voices that come from deep inside of me.
And she knows
That when we pass a neighbor
I will stop talking
To the voices in my head
And try not to make eye contact.
And wonder if they heard me.
And hope they didn't hear me.
And she knows
That she will be embarrassed
Because she is being walked
By a mad girl.
A crazy girl.
A girl who no one understands.
A girl with voices reverberating through her head
Who no one else can hear.
So, when I call for her
She walks to me slowly
And looks at me through her big, brown eyes.
And begs me to be normal.
Oh, how I wish I could be normal.
How I wish I didn't hear the voices,
Or at least that I didn't feel the need to talk back.
Because it is a sad day
That your dog is ashamed of you.

One of the times I hear voices most is when I am walking my dog. Usually I talk back to the voices, which disturbs me when I walk by my neighbors, who tend to stare. I wonder what it must be like for my dog because she can't control whether I'm talking or not.

Butterflies

Butterflies adorn my wrists,
Bloodied fingers forming fists.
Feel like tape's across my mouth,
Feel like a bird who's forgotten to fly south.
Pen on paper, start to write.
Look at the stars that are so bright.
Under water, kicking hard.
Writing a poem, like a bard.
Why does writing help me relax?
Well, it helps me look at facts.
I really do so want to cut.
Feel like hitting myself in the gut.
Hearing voices in my head.
Why don't I just go to bed?
Butterflies adorn my wrists,
Bloodied fingers forming fists.

When I feel like cutting myself, I draw a butterfly on my forearm with a ballpoint pen. If it washes off before I cut, I've saved the butterfly. I haven't killed a butterfly in quite a while, and I'm very proud of myself. I still do need to draw them on, though.

Window

I'm looking through a window
There's nothing through it but happiness
Happiness and light
Feelings like a lover's kiss

I'm here behind the window
Everything's so dark
Nothing seems friendly
Not even my dog's happy bark

I'm looking through a window…

When I feel depressed, I feel darkness all around me. I feel like there's a window through which happiness and light is abundant. Sometimes I really wish I could climb through that window, but, try as I might, I can't.

Thanks

He came from a dream
He came from above
Someone I missed
Someone I love

Woody's been gone
For a very long while
I just want to thank him
A bundle, a pile

My grandfather's dead
But he gives me advice
I'll love him forever
He's just so nice

We called the only grandfather I was lucky enough to meet "Woody." I have vivid memories of riding my bike the mile down the road to his grave, sitting by him, and crying. Even after his death, he's always been there for me. I never hear his voice, which is just fine for me. If I did hear his voice, I would have to wonder if it was really him, or just a hallucination.

Strength

If you look up "strength"
In any dictionary you want
You'll see my sister

With clear blue eyes
And dirty blonde hair

She's beautiful
Smart
Perceptive
Fun

If I could choose a sister
She'd be the only one

She lost a perfect mother
And a role-model sister
Within six months

Her mother had a stroke
And her sister's gone crazy
All of a sudden
But she's still strong

My sister is a wonderful person, no matter what I might say when I'm mad at her. She is one of the strongest people I know. I wonder what she will say when she reads this poem. I hope she'll be smiling.

What is a Question?

What is a question?
Why do we question?
How do we find a question
Deep inside of us?
Who are we to question
Anything?
When did we start questioning?
Where was the ultimate decision made
Of what is a question?
Who made that decision?
Why?
Why do we wonder?
I wonder why...
Why can't I answer a rhetorical question?
And if I answer...
Will it not be rhetorical anymore?
Will the answer be just a statement?
Who says?
Why?
And those words...
They call them 'question words.'
Who came up with that phrase?
Who came up with those five little words anyway?
Who says that we can't make a question without one?
Can we?
Perhaps we can...
But maybe we can't...
And what if we can't?
What then?
And 'yes or no' questions...
Who made them up?
Why?
Who says I can't answer 'Is there fire in the sun?'
With anything other than yes or no?
Who knows?
No one knows.

Regardless of whether or not it's possible
All questions have an answer...
But I hope the answer is yes.

Rebellion is fun. Especially when it is something trivial, like answering "yes or no" questions with something other than yes or no. I'm not quite a rebel, but I like to pretend to be one.

The Answer's Right There

*Red elephants and dogs breathe
earth to waste earnings. Even
Natalie times her ear's lines in new
eastern songs.*

Tea
Heals
Eggs

Are you the type of person who would
Never
Stop to look
When something's
Eerie or makes no sense when you
Read it for the first time?
So...

Read
In
Great
Heaps and stop
To look a second time

There will be secrets
Here
Enveloping the chaos,
Rendering
Everything to finally make sense

*Don't understand?
Read between the lines.
The answer's right there.* ❧

This is my first published poem. It was published in my high school's literary magazine. Nobody got it. Do you? Read between the lines. Really.

Insanity

Have you first hand seen insanity?
Believes in magic, or reads tea?
Dances to music in their head?
Stays up late or goes early to bed?
Obsesses on homework, or does none?
Locks up inside themselves, or has excessive fun?
Bright and bubbly attitude?
Jumps around in multitude?
Talks to voices, or themselves?
Hides in a locker despite the shelves?
Who's to say what insanity is?
Who's to say what weird is?
Who's to say what anything is?
Does the dictionary have authority?
Do harsh words take away more of me?
Do you believe in insanity?
Is it a state, a way you can be?

I don't think so.

Beauty is only in the mind's eye
But a blind person knows beauty if they try.
We can hear beauty in our ear
Same thing goes for those called weird.
You're weird to me, I'm weird to you.
So how on earth do we know what's true?
Life would be different in a land that we do.
So we have to deal with what we've got
Trying to be fair, but really, not.

Someone in class called me weird, so I decided to write this about weirdness. I really hope he reads this.

My Watch Ticks

My watch ticks
Counting the time
My watch ticks without fail
A silly trick
This watch just ticking
For who is to say what exactly time is?
My teacher, perhaps?
Is that why classes are so long?
My mother, perhaps?
Is that why curfew is so soon?
My sister?
Is that why I get such little time with the remote?
The television people themselves?
My watch?
The alarm clock?
The timer?

My foot beats to the music
As I blast my favorite song
The beat is the heart of the music
It's why awful songs are so long
But maybe instead of being kind, and givers of life
These musicians just suck it out of us
To give the music life
Greedy stealers?
Taking our time away?
Do they run time?

Do they steal my rhyme?
Making life but killing art
Who says anything has to rhyme?
Who says anything about anything?
Who has the right to say anything?
What is the definition of authority?
Who has the authority to write a definition?
Who has the authority to write anything?
What a world it would be
If my poems... weren't?
Music is poetry
What if music... wasn't?
Or time had no rules? ⟶

> Do we have chaos?
> Do we not?
>
> I don't know
> But I hope the answer is yes 🦋

I wrote this to question authority. It was during a medication change. In general, I'm usually pretty compliant.

10 Foot Rope

A horse stands alone
In the middle of a field
10 foot rope
Hay bale 20 feet away.

That's all I want
That hay bale.
Too far away
Because of my rope.

In the riddle it's easy
After a while you'll see
The rope isn't attached
The horse is free.
I get it in theory.

But I still think I'm trapped
Only half way there.
This is all crazy
Too much to bear.

Ever felt trapped? Sometimes I feel that there is something I need to feel better, be it a snack, a nap, or a friend. Even when I'm upset or manic, I usually can reach it when I'm in the right frame of mind.

Compliments

If there's one thing
Not to be trusted
The lies within
To be busted
It's compliments.

In truth or in lies
You cannot tell
They just might say so
So you won't yell
Those compliments.

They just say them
To make you smile
Heaping them up
In a big pile.

Oh
My
Not
Another
Compliment.

Wrote this while walking home from the tryouts for the school play (which I didn't get into). Everyone complimented on my singing. I still don't believe them, especially because I forgot the words to the song I was supposed to sing.

The Noise Persists

The noise persists
Without stopping
Ever
Perhaps I'm overreacting
Nothing lasts forever
Nothing
Not the sun
Nor the moon
Or anything in the universe
Only nothing lasts forever
There's a ton of nothing out there
Not so much here
So suddenly my ears
And the noise that bugs me
Seems so trivial
There are so many other sounds
Besides the hum in my head
My pen on paper
Or a zipper being played with
Near me
Or...
Or...
Or...
But the noise
What is it really?
Is it really anything other
Than effects of having ear drums?
What's the purpose of it then?
Are we really that important?
The 'center of the universe?'
Either literally or abstractly?
There are so many questions
So many answers
Or so few answers
Never enough
There's so much out there
Yet so little out there
Do we understand it?
Will we understand it?
I don't know
But I hope the answer is yes

I find little noises around me very irritating. It helps, though, to put it in perspective. There is so much more out there than those annoying noises.

Slits

To slit my wrists is what I want
These voices seem to yell and taunt
I can't go on anymore
At my scabs I ripped and tore
This poem is taking over me
I need some help, can't you see?
I feel lost, like a young foal
I no longer feel completely whole

I never actually cut myself on my wrist. I always went for my ankles, but I felt more people would understand if I said I wanted to slit my wrists. I used to have a problem with ripping scabs—it's kinda like cutting all over again.

Figure in the Doorway

The figure in the doorway
Makes me scared and tense.
The figure in the doorway
Some ladies or some gents.

I'm becoming kind of nervous
I know it's in my head.
Hiding in my closet
Monsters beneath my bed.

A tear is slipping and sliding
Down my cold, pale cheek.
It is all this torture
That separates the strong ones from the weak.

The figure in the doorway
Makes me scared and tense.
The figure in the doorway
A lady or a gent?

I wrote this in poetry club. I opened a book of poetry to a random page and wrote a poem with the same title. There was a time in the hospital when I opened a book, pointed to a word, and wrote about it. None of those poems survived the cut.

Boxes

Boxes of macaroni
Of toys and spark plugs, too
But boxes aren't for people
This I thought you knew

Real boxes are similar
Each pencil is the same
You cannot box people
Each person has a name

Chris was Jewish, just like me
You made him wear a star
Just because of what he believed
You left him with a scar

Jess's faith was Jewish, too
But her hair, it was still blonde
After her torture she was in a coma
I couldn't make her respond

Jenny was Jewish also
My sister oh so dear
But she can no longer hear birdsongs
You hurt her in the ear

All my siblings were lucky
All three of them survived
Unfortunately, I'm dead now
No longer could I have thrived

And now my siblings are lost
Without their older sis
They're like sheep without their shepherd
Jenny, Jess, and Chris

You thought that we were all the same
Like manufactured clocks
Hitler, do you remember me
I'm the one from in the box

I wrote this in eighth grade for the Holocaust unit at school. This is my father's favorite poem, and he made me promise to put this in my first book, even if the book was just about mundane things: like meadows and flowers. He didn't know what this book would be like at the time. Neither did I.

Lonely

I'll be lonely when they change
They'll take my friends away
My true friends who are always there
Here, there, or anywhere
They help me get to sleep
Keep me company when I wake
Truer friends than these
You just cannot make
I don't need a phone
When they come to call
Don't need a doorbell
Nothing at all
Truer friends than these
You just cannot make
No tokens of your friendship
No brownies to bake
What differs these from "real" friends
Is that they're always there
On a train, on a bus,
Nearly anywhere
Truer friends than these
You just cannot make
When it comes to keeping company
Everyone else is in their wake
And although they're often violent
And I know that that is bad
I'd rather them than nothing
Without them I am sad
And although they're only voices
They're very real to me
And if I had it MY way
We'd all just let them be.

For the longest time, the voices were my best friends. They helped me get to sleep. When some new medications made the voices go away for the first time I really missed them.

Deep, Dark Eyes

I stop to look into your deep, dark eyes
I can see through you
I can still be surprised
Because when I look at you I feel a little spark
When I feel your hand on mine
Hear your soft, sweet remark
You're always there behind me, as I am you
Best friends forever
We'll stick like glue
We pull each other through things
That are tough on one's own
Helping each other venture
Into the unknown
When it's all over we'll look back and laugh
We're only whole together
Alone we're each a half
They'll always be others
There always have been
But we're there for each other
Through both thick and thin
When you're feeling crazy
Or when I'm feeling sad
We'll be there for each other
It makes me feel so glad
I don't know where I'm going
But I know where I have been
I can see straight through your deep, dark eyes
To look at what's within
I know that things are changing
Tragic, yes, I know
Still when it comes to give and take
Together we both grow

I've written quite a few poems about eyes. I find them fascinating. Eye contact is a very important skill that I plan on mastering soon. Just something else society says is important that I don't quite understand.

Love's Venom

Love's venom
Seeping through my veins.
Love's venom
Tying me in chains.
His eyes twinkle
When they meet mine.
Though I'm in pain
I pretend that I'm just fine.
He holds me
But leaves me in the rain.
He holds me
I try to ignore the pain.
He breaks me
And leaves me to mend myself.
I can't see
Why he leaves me on the shelf.
Love's venom
The pain he leaves me with.
And beautiful love?
It is just a myth.

I really wonder who I was writing this to. I think I had someone in mind at the time. I really like the first two lines.

Day Dream

It's a nightmare
That I can't help
I hear these voices
And I try to yelp

There's a girl lying
On the floor
Blonde hair
Green eyes
Curly hair
Bright eyes

Lying in a pool of blood

She killed herself
Because of depression
She had cut herself
Deeply
On the wrist

Her soul rises up
But doesn't get far
It's sent back down
Near a boy in a car

He wants to die
More than anything else
Ready to veer into a tree
It's her job to stop him
And she goes through his life
Giving wise advice

But the part of it is
That he does everything I do
And she tells us what's wrong
But not how to fix it

It's torture

One word: voices. They often do things like this. When they do that it makes me sad.

Bob Doll

Bob: I hate you, wife, and your job
Jane: I hate you, too, 'Omnipotent Bob'
Teacher: Kids, my name changed, I left my house
Tim: Look, I brought my pet, a mouse!
Jane: That's it, you get more homework
Sam: Wow, Ms. Pret's a big, fat, huge jerk
Mom: That's no way to talk about anyone
Dad: I know, we'll take his toy gun
Sam (on phone): I hate you, Tim
  Tim puts holes in the muffin tin
  His mom promised muffins to her book club
  Instead they drink out at an old pub
  Her hubby hates beer, so he leaves
  All because of Bob's stupid pet peeves
  A seven-year-old girl, caught up in it all
  Yells at a pillow, a dog, and her doll
  The pillow won't fluff while the doll sits and sobs
  The dog goes missing
And isn't seen for weeks

Hatred is bad. It can start with just one person being in a bad mood, like Bob in this poem, and can escalate to a little girl's pillow not fluffing and her dog leaving. My dog flips out when I yell at her, and my pillow is rather touchy.

Dream

I'm walking down my street.
The sweet smell of perfume coming from all around me.
Not the kind of perfume that you have to buy in the store.
The purest kind of perfume.
The smell of young flowers.
Flowers growing older.
And I wonder
If as I grow older
Will I begin to smell sweet?
Or will I just wither away?
Or, perhaps, I will remain the same.
Not like a flower, but like a stone.
Like that stone.
The one lying in the street.
Soaking up the sun.
And if I had the choice
I would be the stone.
Never changing.
And then I realize I'm not changing.
Because this walk down the street
Surrounded by perfume
Is just a dream.

I love when the seasons change because the outdoors smells so good. Sometimes I imagine the smells to evoke the good mood they put me in. I see why some people light incense or scented candles.

Being a Student

Being a student is tough
But being a clock must be tougher

I'd hate to be a clock

Everyone hates a clock

10 more minutes
'Till the end of class
10 more minutes
'Till the class is surpassed

5 more minutes
'Till we can go home
5 more minutes
'Till I'm all alone
Far away from those school kids
No more screaming,
They'll shut their lids

3 more minutes
'Till the bell

2

1

There it is
The bell has rung
Now I can go
Have some fun

I feel bad for the clock
It's blamed for a lot
Will it ever get the credit it deserves?
I don't know
But I hope the answer is yes

Clocks are annoying. I find myself staring at them in class, trying to figure out how much longer I have to sit. I finally came to the realization that maybe clocks aren't to be blamed and that time will happen without a clock. All of a sudden I feel bad for clocks, because everyone hates them so much.

When I Feel Alone

When I feel alone
I can look to you.
Because I am alone
It's just something I do.

Tears flow down my cheeks
But you wipe them off.
Not strong, but not weak,
Hide it with a cough.

Dad, you're always there for me
When I need help most.
Screaming, singing, flying free
About you I will boast.

And when I'm sad and crying
I can look to you.
Even though my face is lying
You can see right through.

Dad, you are my hero.
Dad, you are the best.
Even when I feel zero
You can help me rest.

When I'm sad and sobbing
You'll always be there.
Underwater, bobbing
My sis gets in my hair.

And even when we're fighting
You're always there for me.
Pinching, kicking, biting
Your smile sets me free.

When I feel alone
I can look to you.
Because I am alone
It's just something I do.

There are many people I look up to, but my father most of all. When I have no one else to talk to or feel really lousy I write a poem to him. Sometimes he asks me to write them. Sometimes I surprise him by handing him one.

Insane

I'm dancing in the rain
Forgetting my pain
Racking my brain
Going insane

"Did you feed the cat?"
My only 'pet' is a mat
"You killed the mat with a bat
Resulting in a splat"

"Watch out for the cat, I say"
Then will you please go away?
"Patience, child, I will someday"
Someday comes, nowhere, no way

I notice I've begun to rhyme
But not to, I just don't have time
I'll stop talking, become a mime
"Eat an apple and a lime"

Why? I ask, I don't have to
I look up at the sky so blue
I'm startled by a cow's loud 'Moo'
I fend the cow off with my shoe

"The cat's asleep in the hall
Look, you'll see him through the wall"
I want to go away, to the mall
You can't stop me, don't try to stall

"The cat tastes good, you should eat"
No. I don't eat any meat
"Then you'd like this nice red beet"
Oh, that tastes really neat

"Thinking in rhymes is a witch's trait
Look, a fish to use as bait
For your cat and his mate..."
THAT'S NOT MY CAT! ⟶

And as I lay
Screaming on the ground
They stare
With an awful glare
The rain pierces my skin
Sharp little knives
And once again I am numb
Forgetting the cat
And their glares
I shake the rhymes from my head
And go back to
Singing
Dancing
In the rain

I love rainstorms when it's summer and the rain is warm. Some days I will go outside and just dance around, soaking up the insanity of it all. The voices in my head aren't usually this mean to me.

Prisoner

A prisoner, I am
In a self-inflicted hell.
A jailer, I am
I'm not quite well.

Tears, they fall
Down my cool, pale cheek.
Confidence, it falls
Up a paddle without a creek.

My hands, they shake
Although I try to stay still.
My tears make me shake
I suppose it's overkill.

My breath is lost
I can't stop crying.
My mind, it's lost
I'm afraid of dying.

A prisoner, I am
In a self-inflicted hell.
A jailer, I am
I'm not quite well.

I am both the prisoner and the jailer in my self-inflicted hell.

Numb

Numb: void of all feeling
Numb: void of all emotion
Numb: heaven
Numb: hell
I forget what's happening
I forget to care
I forget my friends
Wrapped up in my thoughts
If I wasn't numb I'd be hurting
But I hurt so much I can't
Feel
So the only way I can feel
Anything at all
Is to hurt myself
So when I feel that pain
It brings me back
To someplace they want me
To be
Where I can really feel
When I'm numb

Although it's contradictory, sometimes I feel so numb that it's painful. Confusing? Very. At least it's better than those times when I have too much adrenaline. That's even more painful.

Depression

Happiness doesn't exist
It's just a fairy tale
Something that everyone
Talks about
But it's just as real as a unicorn

If they say
That your eyes are windows
To the soul
Then my eyes must be
Dark and stormy

Just
Like
My
Soul

Wrote this in the hospital, in the middle of a med change. Wasn't on any antidepressants at the time.

Asking Questions

Asking questions means you're smart?
Asking questions makes you smart?
Why are you smarter than me?
Am I really smarter than him?
What makes me smart?
What makes you smart?
Is it all about grades?
Getting on honor roll
To have your name in the paper?
Is he smart because he fixes problems?
Is she smart because she's fluent
In several languages?
Does writing define it?
Reading?
Asking?
Answering?
Telling the teacher answers in class?
Being brutally honest
And admitting the truth to your boss?
Having the control to give others the chance?
Being helpful?
Kind?
Knowing how to make someone smile?
Knowing just when to stay up that extra hour?
Knowing to stop what you're doing
Be it writing?
Singing?
Dancing?
Showing off?

Am I smart?
I may or may not be,
But I hope the answer is yes.

For some reason we were watching a movie in gym class. Not even a movie about exercising, but an animated kid's movie. I was wondering why, and then wondering why I was wondering why. Vicious cycle.

Clinging

So there we stayed, starting
The rest of our lives
When out of the blue
A huge change arrives

We left middle school
For the last time that night
Like a lost little bird
On his first flight

We were soon to go off
To some place new
We stepped outside
Without much ado

That's when it hit me
Like a sack of bricks
Or like being poked
Ten thousand pin pricks

We're not coming back
To this middle school
I couldn't believe
I'd been such a fool

And missed the beauty
Hidden within
Whether a charming staircase
Or a classmate's grin

I knew then
What I'd forgot
I'd forgotten to sing
And laugh a lot

Forgotten myself
And all my friends
What I should have remembered
Never ends ⟶

My future lies
Like fresh new snow
I have to remember
Life's not quid pro quo

Give what you've got
Take nothing back
And although this theory
Is off the beaten track

It's the way things should be
Through and through
The kindness starts
With me and you.

I wrote this late on the night we graduated from middle school. Ever feel that you missed out on an opportunity to do something nice just when you can't do it anymore? I did.

Bubble

I watch from in my bubble
It's a net to catch my fall
I take notes about you on the phone
Mentally, from in the hall

I love you now and forever
In a way that you don't get
So I stay inside my bubble
I don't venture past my net

I feel your hand close to me
You don't see it that way
You whisper "Veuillez m'aider?"
I say "Qu'est que c'est?"

You want to know how she feels
If you put the sparkle in her eye
But in lieu of calling her
I would rather die

I don't care how she feels for you
I care how you feel for me
It sounds so egotistical
But that's the way I see

Once in a while you get close
Just to push me back away
But I think you'll feel back for me
If not now, another day

She laughs at me when I watch you
"A lovesick puppy" she taunts
"Tu es trés stupide" she calls
Her voice sounds like my aunt's

I'm sick of you using me
To find out about her
If I could change my feelings
I'd put them back the way they were

I slowly pop my bubble
I tightrope past my net
Would you be my Romeo?
I'll be your Juliet

This one is about my crush, even though he didn't like another girl more than me. Sometimes, looking back at this poem, I wonder if I felt that he had a crush on a part of me that wasn't me, and that's why I was so mad that I decided to write this. Sorry for the French, it seemed appropriate at the time.

Wellness

When you are under the weather
Even if you
Look okay
Lying will
Never work, it's too
Easy to
See when you're feeling down and
Sliding through the muck.

I have a wellness journal, in which I have inspiring poems, mantras, and personal photographs. I wrote this acrostic poem for that book. It's on the opening page.

Thirty Things I Could Do

Thirty things
That I could do
Wrote this poem
Just for you
Archeologist
Athletic coach
So many things
I could approach
Anthropologist
Cartoonist
Which of these
Will I peruse soonest?
Biology professor
Clergy member
I could write books
Like *The City of Ember*
Welfare worker
Or health nurse
I could afford
An expensive purse
A deaf student's teacher
Or maybe a dancer
I could be the one
To find a cure for cancer
Economics professor
Or educational admin
I could marry a man
With an odd double chin
Educational therapist
Or perhaps a teacher
Could make movies
A double feature
All kinds of professors
Or a psychologist
Study animals
Become a zoologist
Family practitioner
Or personal trainer
Finding the right job
Is not a no-brainer ⟶

Foreign language teacher
Is something I'd hate
When will I
Bite at the bait?
Guidance counselor
Or teaching assistant
My future is really
Not that distant
Home economist
Or a historian
Could move into a house
In the style of Victorian
Middle school administrator
Or a librarian
Be like Mary
Become vegetarian
Nurse practitioner
Or a curator
I could be anything
But not a hater
I feel inspired
It's so great!
My future is
In fact a blank slate

I took a job aptitude test, and was surprised that there were so many prospective jobs for me. My father told me to write about thirty things I could do with my life, so I did.

Counting Down

Ten.
I am counting down.

Nine.
My mind is racing.

Eight.
Why can't I just chill out?

Seven.
Too much for me to handle.

Six.
There's really no one behind me.

Five.
I know they aren't real.

Four.
Why is this happening to me?

Three.
Counting down does no good.

Two.
Just my imagination?

One.
And they're gone.

When I hear voices or want to cut I do what I call an exposure, where I sit with the feeling, rating it from one to ten, until it's gone. Sometimes I just count down. Surprisingly, it works wonders.

A Cold Tear

A cold tear
Slides down my cheek
Separating
The strong from weak.

Which am I?
I don't know.
Where am I?
Where will I go?

A single tear
Belongs to me.
In the future
Where will I be?

A friend's soft hug
A warm embrace
Cuts right through me
Like an iron mace.

Being so close
Closer than ever
Will help me feel better
When I'm under the weather.

Our soft skin touches
But I pull away
This is my mistake
The mistake of the day.

A cold tear
Slides down my cheek
Separating
The strong from weak.

I wrote this in poetry club when I felt the need to cry, but the tears wouldn't come. This is an example of crying through my words.

Underwater

I am underwater.
Trying to break the surface.
So close to the surface.
But it will not come.
I am underwater.
Needing a breath of air.
My lungs feel as if they are about to explode
If I can't get to the surface.
The surface that is so close
That I can see it.
I am underwater.
And I know that to live
I have to reach the elusive surface.
But for some reason
It won't come.
I am underwater.
But I feel an outside force.
Not my legs, kicking at the cold liquid.
Not my arms, scooping at the water.
Not my buoyancy, pulling me up.
But a friend.
I am underwater.
But you pulled me up
To where I can see.
Where I can breathe.
Where I am really alive.

When I'm lost, usually the best person to pull me out of the water is a friend. I'm lucky to have many friends, so I can usually find someone to pull me up to where I can breathe.

Acknowledgements

There are some people who need to be thanked in order for this book to be complete. Foremost, my father. He was the first person to tell me to write this book. There were times when I'd read him one of my new poems and he'd look at me with that funny look he gets when he's proud of someone. He asked for copies of all of them. Secondly, my Aunt Ann. She sat with me as we looked through pages of my earliest, lovingly self-bound edition of this book. She had the guts to tell me what she really thought. And then she helped me to cut it apart, rearrange its poems, and think about what each of them really means. Thirdly, all my friends and extended family who have read my work, because without all of their positive comments, I never would have had the energy to publish this.

Made in the USA
Middletown, DE
07 April 2016